RIGHT FIELD RULERS

Building Defense and Power in Right Field

Strategies, Skills, and Success

SKY BENSON

TABLE OF CONTENTS

CHAPTER 1

RIGHT FIELD FOUNDATIONS

Understanding your responsibilities

"And role."

Picture this: the crack of the bat breaks the afternoon silence like a rocket soaring into the farthest right Field. It's a crucial moment that can make or break the game. It tests your skills, focus, and knowledge of the right fielder's important part. First, talk about what it means to be a right fielder: the leader of your defensive area. Then you can catch that line drive or run back for that giant fly ball. It would help if you did more than watch over an open outfield area as a right fielder. As an outfielder, you need to be like a quiet guardian who sees danger coming and stops it with a diving catch or a laser throw. It's about knowing how to communicate and execute flawlessly with your teammates while staying in sync with your place.

It's essential to communicate.

Baseball has many moving parts, and the right fielder is in charge of the orchestra in the outfield. It is imperative to stay in touch with the centerfielder. A simple "I got it!" or "Play shallow!" can keep the fielding process from bumping into anything and running smoothly. The catcher also turns into an essential source of details. You can predict plays and set yourself up carefully if you know the signs about pitch types and possible baserunners.

"Master of Your Zone"

Your main job is to control the area between the foul line in the right Field and a specific part of the centerfield. Usually, you can find out what that area is by talking to the centerfielder before the game. This zone is your kingdom, and you have to be very careful all the time to control it. It becomes second nature to judge fly balls; your eyes follow the ball's path, and your feet move naturally to meet it at its peak. The fielder must have quick reflexes and a smooth stance to catch and throw a ground ball quickly to the infield.

Getting Used to the Game

But the right fielder's job isn't just catching fly and ground balls. You always have to be able to change with the game. Shifts, which are changes in defensive positioning based on the batter, need quick thought. One second, you could be deep in the outfield; the next, you could be creeping in to catch a possible line drive. It is imperative to know these defense alignments and be able to switch between them without any problems.

More Than the Basics

Do you think the right fielder's job ends when the last batter strikes out? Not quite. It's essential to back up throws from the infield on bunts and bunts. You protect the first baseman by ensuring that a dropped throw doesn't give the other team an extra base. In the same way, the shortstop or third baseman needs to back up throws on balls hit to the left side of the Field so that a base hit doesn't turn into a double.

How a right fielder thinks

You need a unique set of skills to play the right Field. Wearing well requires a strong arm, running fast to catch fly balls, and bending over and seeing them. But it's also about being tough mentally. Staying focused on the game is essential, even when you're not doing anything. What makes a good baseball player great is their ability to deal with pressure, especially when men are on base, and the game is on the line.

Being a right fielder means knowing your job and your importance to the defense. It's about getting good at your zone, talking to people clearly, and changing with the game as it goes on. It's about staying focused and always wanting to get better. Taking the Field means you own the area around the right Field and are in charge of the defense.

Fielding techniques

"For ground balls and fly balls."

The right Field isn't just a pretty grass area; it's a battlefield where speed and skill meet. A right fielder's main job is catching ground and fly balls. Doing these things well sets good fielders apart from great ones. Let's examine the critical skills that will turn you from a bystander to a defense powerhouse.

Basics of Ground Ball

You must respond quickly and keep your body still when you're a grounder. Keep your center of gravity low. Let's say you're ready to make a jump shot in basketball. This lets you get to the ball faster and gives you a more stable base for handling. As soon as the ball leaves the bat, could you keep your eyes on it? Don't be fooled by the batter's swing or the ball's first path. Pay close attention to where the ball goes and let your body respond naturally. How you walk is very important. Don't take giant steps to catch the ball. Take short, choppy steps instead of a long, slow walk to get to the ball. This makes it easier to keep your balance and make quick changes when the ground ball hops out of the green. This is "The Glove Whisperer." It would help if you were friends with your glove. Hold it comfortably in front of you with the bottom edge pointing down. Keep it open and your fingers pointing down to make a funnel that will catch the ball safely. As you move toward the ball, slightly extend your hand in front of your body when the ball hits the ground. If the ball takes a bad hop, this "scooping" action will ensure you catch it cleanly. Do not focus on the netting; catch the ball in your glove pocket. Moving the ball quickly to your throwing hand is essential once you have the ball in your hand. You can make a strong throw by rapidly moving the glove to your throwing hand and putting the ball on your fingers.

Getting Good at the Fly Ball

When you hit a fly ball, you must focus on tracking and catching instead of being quick. As soon as the ball leaves the bat, make a mental note of where it's going. It would be best to guess where the ball would land by looking at the angle and distance. For an easy catch, this lets you get under the ball when it's at its highest point. As you watch the fly ball, keep your place under the ball by backpedaling slowly. Keep your eyes on the ball, and don't run backward. Instead, shuffle or backpedal quickly. Does a crow hop to get a little higher before catching the ball? With this hop, you can reach for higher fly balls because it lets you extend your hand. It's essential to jump with your throwing leg, land on your glove-side leg first, and then move your weight to your throwing leg if you need to make a strong throw. "The Catch" means putting your hand out with a firm but controlled grip as the ball falls. Keep both hands on the ball as you catch it in your glove pocket. Let the ball come to you, take the hit, and make the catch. Don't try to stop it. The most important thing is to talk to each other. If you see another player coming toward the fly ball, call it off so that no one gets hit. A simple "I got it!" can stop something terrible from happening.

Making Practice Better

It takes time to get good at these methods. It's important to train regularly. Work with a partner who can throw ground balls at different speeds and directions. Work on your shuffle strategy, fielding skills, and throwing techniques. Play catch with a fungo bat or a ball launcher and hit fly balls of different lengths and heights. Get better at catching, backpedaling, and the crow hop. Hit fly balls against a wall to work on your spotting. As you hit the ball against the wall from different directions, please pay attention to how it bounces and how to catch it at the peak.

You can do more than look at the view in the right Field. It's a tough defense spot that needs commitment and concentration. You can become a confident and reliable right fielder who can turn any ground ball or fly ball into an out if you learn these fielding methods and put in the practice time.

Perfecting your throwing mechanics

"For accuracy and strength."

The sound of the bat hitting the ball. A fiery line drive hurtles toward the gap. You feel pumped with energy; it's time to fire the cannon. If you play right Field, your weapon is a robust and precise throw. It can make the difference between an extra-base hit and an exciting out. How do you turn raw strength into a throw that always hits its mark? Let's learn about the art and science of throwing physics to ensure your throws are solid and accurate.

Getting to Know the Mechanics

An excellent way to throw is like a complicated dance where all the moves are coordinated. Getting a good grip on the ball is the first critical step. A four-seam grip is excellent for people who throw with their right hand. Set your thumb on the back of the ball and run your middle finger across its edges. This grip gives you good speed and control. This part of the throw provides you with speed. Step back with your other leg (the left leg for right-handed throwers), and bring your throwing hand back behind your head so the elbow is high and directed at the target. When you finish a step, your core muscles make your body curve like a spring. This builds up energy that will come out during the throw. Picture yourself holding a tennis ball between your shoulder blades. This is the power step for "The Arm Extension." Let go of your body and forcefully extend your throwing arm forward. When you let go, the arm should end in a straight line toward your goal. Your elbow should lead the way. After you throw the ball, don't stop. Do it with your whole body and step forward with your front foot to keep your balance and control. When you're done throwing, your arm should be pointing at your target.

It is essential to be accurate.

Strength is necessary, but precision is the most important thing. Please keep your eyes on your target, whether the fielder's glove or the base, from when you wind up until you let go. This allows you to aim your throw and keeps the ball moving straight. Good movement gives you a stable base from which to throw. When you let go, your front foot should be pointed toward your goal, and your stride should be balanced. If your upper body is tense, you could lose control. When you throw the ball, keep your shoulders loose and your grip on the ball free.

Getting Stronger

It's not by chance that you have a strong arm for throwing. This is a traditional drill where you and a partner throw the ball farther and farther. Start with a shorter journey and slowly make it longer as your fitness level rises. Add weighted balls to your practice for throwing. Without these balls, your muscles would not get as strong over time. Use lighter weights and pay attention to your form to avoid getting hurt. Resistance bands can help you get more robust in the muscles you use for throwing. For movements that work your shoulders, triceps, and core, use them.

Taking it to the Field

To get good at throwing, you must be dedicated and practice regularly. Warm-up: Always remember how important it is to do a good warm-up. You can get your body ready to throw without hurting it by doing light exercises, dynamic stretches, and arm circles. During practice, don't just throw hard; work on throwing correctly. Being consistent and accurate will easily make you go faster. Think about creating a perfect throw by picturing each step of the process. This thought practice can help you concentrate and feel more sure of yourself during the game.

You can make your throws a powerful tool on the Field by learning to throw correctly, focusing on accuracy, and getting stronger. A solid and accurate throw isn't just about winning games; it's also about making your team feel confident and your opponents scared. Take the Field, fire up the gun, and become a right fielder whose throws are as famous as their catches.

CHAPTER 2

PLAYING THE BOUNDARY

Strategies for handling balls

"Hit near the foul line."

The foul line on the right Field is skinny and hard to avoid. It separates fairground from an annoying out. As a right fielder, balls hitting close to this line are challenging. They need quick reactions, good positioning, and clear communication to make a great defensive play out of a tricky situation. How can you become a master of the foul line frontier? Let's look into it.

Reading the Ball

To deal with a foul line screamer, you must first predict its path correctly. Pay close attention to how the batter stands. Is a pull hitter with the right hand at the plate? A foul line drive is more likely to happen. Knowing how the batter usually hits the ball, you can guess where it will go. Don't be fooled by the angle of take-off at first. It's incredible how quickly a ball that looks like it's going foul can hook back into a fair area. Keep your eyes on the ball's whole path. When there is a foul line, the wind is significant. A strong wind from right Field can bring a ball back into play that looks like it should be out of play. On the other hand, a strong wind can send a fair ball toward the foul line.

Setting up your situation

To handle foul line shots, you need to be strategically placed. It depends on the situation whether you should be shallow or deep. Are you being hit by a powerful batter known for hitting foul balls far? Give the ball a little more room to run and catch it. If the batter makes more contact and throws the ball more evenly, stopping line drives in a deeper position might be better. It is imperative to talk to the centerfielder. A simple shout like "I got it!" or "Play shallow!" can keep players from running into each other and keep the defense running smoothly. Pay attention to what the judge says. You can change where you are based on the absolute path of the ball if they call a foul early.

Putting on the Play

After figuring out where you want to be and where the ball is going, it's time to make the play. Quickly move if the ball goes back into the fair area. Maintain your place under the ball with a smooth backpedal, then catch the ball correctly to get out. The ball can sometimes touch the foul line, making it a close call. In this case, run as fast as possible to the ball and try to catch it by jumping. You can get an out by moving the ball back into the infield, even if you don't see it. When it comes to playing it safe, there are times when it's best to do nothing. Stop a base hit first if you're unsure if the ball will stay fair or foul. If the ball remains fair, run straight to the foul line to give yourself the best chance of finding it and making a play on it.

High-Level Strategies

If it looks like the ball will go foul, you can use a fake retreat to get the runner to move forward. As if you were giving up the ball, take a few steps back and then quickly charge forward to make a play if it dips back into a fair area. Before you catch a ball that might touch the foul line, you can move your glove a little into the fair area. This makes it more likely that the ball will stay fair, even if it barely touches the foul line. Be careful, though, and only use this strategy to avoid an umpire's call.

Making Practice Better

To get good at foul line situations, you have to train hard. Have a coach or partner hit fungo fly balls that go in different directions, with some going over the foul line. This helps you get better at reading the ball and making changes. Have a buddy stand next to the foul line and throw fly balls at you from different angles to make it look like you're inside it. Learn how to catch and throw while running. Place cones along the foul line to show different depths of placement. Running from one cone to the next will help you prepare for game situations where you must change your place quickly.

Getting Good at the Mental Game

Situations with foul lines can be scary. Don't let the stress get to you. Keep your attention on the ball's path and trust the placement and communication you did before the game. Take deep breaths and stay relaxed and sure of yourself. Trust your instincts; you've been through this many times before. When the ball is hit, go with your gut and do what comes easily. Doubting yourself can make you hesitate and miss out on chances. Every time you get called for a foul, you can learn something. Look at both the plays that worked and the ones that didn't. What went well? How could you have done it better? Use what you've learned to get better at your game.

You can become a great right fielder who loves playing on the edge if you learn these techniques, know how to position yourself well, and keep calm under pressure. The foul line won't be scary; instead, it will be a chance to show off your skills and turn a possible trouble into a highlight-reel catch. The foul line in Right Field is more than just a line; it's your playground where you can show off your defensive skills and become the absolute master of Right Field.

Making plays on the wall

"And understanding the ballpark's dimensions."

A considerable fly ball sails straight at you, making a beautiful arch against the clear blue sky. The crowd's cheers get louder. People who love baseball will never forget the right fielder running back, making a desperate leap at the wall and the gasp as his glove hits the leather to save the game. But making plays at the wall isn't just about being brave; it's also about knowing your ballpark, guessing where the ball will go, and learning techniques to get out. Let's learn about outfield walls, which will turn you from a bystander to a brave defender on the edge of the pitch.

Getting to Know Your Ballpark

Each ballpark is different, like a person with their attitude. Right fielders need to know their home venue and every other ballpark they play in. They know how high the walls are in different parts of the right Field. Is there more space between the right Field and the right center? These changes can make or break your chances of making a play at the wall. Watch out for the foul area past the wall. There are insufficient grounds that go deep in some parks and walls that rise right up from the stands in others. Knowing how far the wall is from the stands, you can figure out how deep the ball is and whether you can make a leaping play. Different wall angles can create strange situations. Balls hitting a few feet off the ground might look like they are in play if the wall has a slight tilt toward the inside. Knowing these details will help you make more accurate predictions about where the ball will go.

How to do Wall Plays

It takes specific skills and a lot of guts to get good at wall plays. From the moment the ball leaves the bat, keep your eyes on it. Don't be fooled by its original path; a high-fly ball can trick you with a long hang time. Quickly figure out how far the wall is and where you think the ball will land. Make the necessary changes to your speed to reach the wall just as the ball hits its highest point. As you move toward the wall, keep your backpedal steady, a series of short, quick steps. This lets you make changes and keeps you from running over the ball. Do a substantial jump before reaching the wall to get as far as possible. Make sure you jump at the right time and focus on achieving your glove hand as high as possible. Watch out for the wall padding as you jump. Lean a little toward the wall to protect yourself from getting hurt when the ball hits you. For "The Secure Catch," keep your hand closed and firm when you hit the ball. Don't make a mistake because you're excited.

First Safety

Making plays at the wall is fun, but safety comes first. Don't try to catch something that you can't safely reach. It could be dangerous to hit the wall. If you're not sure what to do, play the ball off the wall for a ground rule double. Always talk to your teammates, primarily the centerfielder. Tell them you're going for the wall to keep from running into them. Set aside time before the game to do good warm-ups and stretching exercises. During wall play, loose muscles are more likely to get hurt.

Making Practice Better

It would help if you practiced them for hours to get good at wall plays. Find a safe wall and practice jumping and catching the ball against it. Start with throws that stay in place and work up to throws that change speed and angle over time. As a partner wall drill, have a friend throw fly balls at a wall to make it feel like a real game. Work on jumping, backpedaling, and making catches. Get better at figuring out how far fly balls go. Hit fly balls from different distances with a partner or a coach to simulate hitting the wall in various ways.

After the Catch

Making a great catch at the wall is exciting, but the work isn't done yet. Hold on tight to the ball once you've caught it. Don't get so excited that you lose the ball, which could give the runner an extra base if you can. Turn around immediately and throw the ball back to the infield. You can use the speed from your jump to make a strong throw that might catch a runner trying to tag up. Let your friends know about the out and pass along any information you have about possible baserunners. If you and your friends all do a quick fist pump after a good catch, it will boost morale.

How to Get Over Your Wall Mentality

Making plays at the wall takes more than just physical skill. Have faith that you can make the catch. When you're sure of yourself, you make quick decisions and are ready to go all out for the out. Wall plays are fine to use. Think of them as chances to show off your skills and make a play that changes the game. Look at every wall play, whether you make the ball or not. What went well? How could you have done it better? Use what you've learned to make your next tries better.

By learning the dimensions of your ballpark, mastering wall play skills, putting safety first, and developing a positive attitude, you can go from being a right fielder who watches to a brave wall guard. Not worrying about those huge fly balls; instead, they'll be chances to make baseball history with a jaw-dropping catch or a game-saving play. You can show off your speed and bravery at the outfield wall, which is more than just a wall. It's the edge of your defensive area. Take charge of your right Field, enjoy the task, and learn how to master the wall.

Practicing specific drills

"For challenging catches."

As a right fielder, what makes your game great is the thrill of the chase. However, not every catch is the same. A screaming line drive may require a diving jump, while a high-flying ball may need a wall jump timed just right. These difficult saves separate the good from the great, turning a disaster into a moment for the highlight reel. But how do you get better at grabs and master even the hardest ones? Let's do some drills to help you improve at those tricky catches.

Putting down a foundation

Ensure you grasp basic fielding skills well before moving on to more challenging drills. Learn how to move for ground and backpedal with control for fly balls. For glove work, hold the ball comfortably and securely in all situations. Practice catching soft fly balls and grounders with one hand to improve glove control. For solid and accurate throws after a catch, focus on proper throwing form with a smooth follow-through.

Beating the Diving Catch

When someone dives to catch a ball, they show strength and bravery. To do the Superman Slide, find a flat piece of grass. Take a running jump forward, falling headfirst with your arms stretched out. This is called a sprinter's stance. Rolling onto your side to absorb the force is a safe way to practice landing. Have a partner throw grounders and line drives at different speeds and angles. This is called "Partner Throw and Dive." It would help if you worked on running as fast as possible to the ball, jumping to catch it, and ensuring your glove is tight around it. Please set up a line of cones to make it look like a ground ball situation. As you run to the cones, practice sliding or diving at each one, paying attention to where your glove goes and how well you catch the ball.

How to Master the Backhanded Catch

You must be quick and have a smooth glove transfer for the backhanded catch. This is called "Soft Toss Backhand." Have a partner throw fly balls slightly to your right, so you must reach back with your glove to grab them. Start throwing slowly and build up your strength as you feel more comfortable. Catch fly balls with only your glove hand against a wall or with a partner to practice a backhanded catch in a game setting. Do running drills and backhand catches at the same time. While you jog backward, have a person throw you fly balls. Then, switch to a backhanded catch at the top of the ball's path.

How to Tame the Wall Ball

The wall can help you or hurt you. To do a wall jump catch, find a safe, padded wall. Focus on getting your glove as high as possible when you jump straight up while standing close. As your confidence grows, slowly move farther away from the wall. Have a person stand next to the wall and throw fly balls at different heights and angles to make it feel like a game. Backpedal, jump and make catches against the wall to improve your skills. Hit fly balls at a wall from different distances with a partner or coach. Get better at figuring out how deep the ball is and when to jump to make a perfect wall catch.

Readiness for Mind

A lot of physical work is only half the fight. Before a game or practice, close your eyes and picture yourself making a flying catch, a wall grab while jumping, or a smooth backhanded snare. Pay attention to the steps, enjoy the results, and boost your confidence. Don't let the nerves before the game take your attention away. Please pay close attention to each task during practice to make it feel like a game. "Embrace the Challenge" means to push yourself during drills. Change how fast and how hard you throw to push yourself and gain the courage to handle any catch that comes your way.

After the Drills

Not only at the drill field but also in real life. Watch clips of right fielders making tough catches. Look at their timing, skill, and how they're standing and sitting. Take what the best players have taught you and use it in your own game. To master difficult catches, you need to have solid legs and a strong core. As part of your workout program, do exercises that work on these areas. Have faith that you can make the catch. To get over your fear of failing and make those risky plays, you need to keep an upbeat attitude.

You can go from being a nervous watcher to a right fielder who loves the unexpected by doing these drills, building mental toughness, and always looking for ways to improve. You won't have to worry about those screaming line drives and towering fly balls; they'll be chances to show off your agility and make a play that leaves the crowd gasping. The right Field is more than just a big green area; it's your challenge zone. This is where your hard work and skill meet to turn chaos into confidence and make you an absolute master of the grab. Put on your cleats, walk out onto the Field, and enjoy the thrill of the run. The following catch that will go down in history books could be yours.

CHAPTER 3

OFFENSIVE POWER

Hitting techniques

"For consistency and power."

The sound of the bat hitting the ball. That good sting in your hands. The thrill of a perfect hit in baseball is unmatched: a high-line drive that splits the outfield. But brute force isn't the only way to get constant contact and raw power. To become a hitting machine, you must learn the complicated dance of hitting mechanics, where timing and technique meet. Let's look at the most important things that will improve your hitting and turn you from a hopeful swinger into a fearsome force at the plate.

The Base: A Stance of Balance

For a powerful swing, you need a strong base. Keep your feet shoulder-width apart and put equal weight on both balls of your feet. People often use the "closed stance," meaning that your front foot is slightly turned toward the pitcher. This makes a stable base for producing electricity. Keep your back straight and bend your knees just a little. Don't bend or lean forward; keep your back straight and loose. Hold the bat comfortably on the top hand grip of your dominant hand, with your bottom hand about a hand's width below. Relax your grip; a death grip makes it hard to control the bat.

The Load and the Stride

The "load" and "stride" are critical parts starting the spin. As the pitcher begins to wind up, do a small backward load by twisting your body and moving your weight back a little. This builds up energy that will be let out during the swing. Slowly step forward with your front foot when the pitcher throws the ball. This step helps you move your weight and speed into the swing. Instead of lunging, try to take a smooth, steady step.

"The Swing: Getting Power Out"

The swing is where everything you've learned fits together. This is where power comes from. When you start to hit, quickly turn your hips toward the pitcher. Think of your core muscles as springs that coil and then release. Pay attention to keeping your bat level as you hit the ball. You might get substantial flyouts when you swing with an uppercut, but you might get weak grounders when you swing with a dip. A level swing that hits the ball straight on is what you should aim for. Don't stop once you touch someone. Finish your swing by stretching your arms and following through with your body. Your bat should now be pointing toward the other Field. If you follow through, you can be sure your power goes into the swing.

Getting in Touch: The Key to Being Consistent

It's fun to hit for power, but a good hitter needs to make steady contact. Pay attention to the pitch and follow the ball from the pitcher's hand to the plate. Don't be tricked by a pitcher's trick delivery; pay attention to where the ball is going and change your swing to match. Taking a big swing is tempting, but you should focus on hitting hits. Avoid pitches too far outside your strike zone, and wait for the right one to let your swing go. Bat speed is essential for getting power and making good contact. Do bat speed workouts to speed up your swing as part of your practice routine.

Making Practice Better

To get good at hitting, you have to keep practicing. Do some simple tee work drills to start. Practice using the proper swing mechanics to hit the ball regularly in different parts of the Field. For the front toss, have a person throw a Fungo bat at you while you practice hitting. Doing this lets you focus on timing and getting contact when live pitching. Do "Mirror Drills," where you practice your swing before a mirror. This enables you to find any mistakes in your form and fix them.

After Mechanics: The Mental Game

Hitting isn't just about being strong physically; it's also about being tough mentally. Avoid all distractions and keep your laser-like attention on the pitcher and the next pitch. Positive Visualization: Before you step up to the plate, picture yourself hitting the ball. Think about the physics, the contact, and the thrill of winning. Break down every at-bat, even if you don't hit a home run. What went well? How could you have done it better? Make changes to your technique and get better at hitting the next time you go up to bat.

More advanced techniques

As you get better at hitting, you can try more advanced techniques to make your game better:

Hitting Different Types of Pitches: Learn how to change your swing for fastballs, curve balls, and change-ups. Pay attention to the type of pitch the pitcher is throwing and make small changes to your swing to make the best contact.

"Choking Up": If you need more control over the bat, you might want to "choke up" on it. You can get more control by moving your grip a couple of inches closer to the end of the bat. If you want to hit the ball to the other side, don't be afraid to do it. This can catch defenders off guard and lead to hits that were not expected.

It takes a lifetime to get good at hitting. There will be bad games, slumps, and difficult times. You can go from being a frustrated swinger to a steady and robust hitter by focusing on the basics, keeping a positive attitude, and always looking for improvement. We are still working on getting the perfect swing. Enjoy the trip, take pleasure in the learning process, and be proud of every success, no matter how small. You'll find your hitting groove and become a massive threat at the plate if you work hard and love what you do. Feel good about your swing as you walk up to the plate, and let the bat hitting the ball be your symphony of victory.

Smart base running

"And situational awareness."

The sound of the bat hitting the ball. You're on first, your heart racing as a blur of options appears. Do you steal second? Are you ready for a double? Your choice could make all the difference at this point in the game. But running the bases-wise isn't just about getting stolen bases. It's about knowing what's going on, making intelligent decisions, and testing the defense to its limits. We will teach you the art of baserunning, turning you from a timid runner into a strategic weapon on the basepaths.

The Base: Being Aware of Your Situation

Before taking a base, you need to know what might happen. In the bottom of the ninth inning, when the score is only one run, you need a different approach than when the score is ten runs in the second inning. Knowing the score and how many games are left helps weigh the risks and benefits. Pay attention to how the pitcher throws the ball. Does he have runners on? Does he have a slow windup that could make it easy to steal? It can help to know how the pitcher usually does things. A team might leave a hole for a steal if a team plays a shift. Pay attention to where the fielders are placed and exploit any defense holes. Stealing a base is less dangerous when there are two outs. The defense is focused on getting the third out, making the steal more likely to go through.

Aggressive base running is what comes after stealing.

Stealing bases is fun, but there's more to intelligent baserunning than just stealing extra bags. Get strong leads off base to make the pitcher work harder and throw more strikes. To predict throws and steal an extra base when the chance comes up, learn secondary leads. Always watch for chances to get extra bases on a wild pitch, a passed ball, or a slow grounder. Push the defenders to make perfect throws as you run down the line. If the batter is moving slowly, you might want to ask the pitcher to make drawing throws to break up his flow and make his arm tired. In later at-bats, this can help your partner at the plate.

Making the Right Choice

Knowing when to be bold and when to play it safe is imperative. What is your base running speed? Are you a fast runner on the base tracks or more cautious? Finding out your skills and weaknesses will help you determine how aggressive you are. If there is a fast runner on base behind you, stealing a base can give you a chance to do a double steal and put pressure on the defense. Any catcher who isn't strong enough to throw out runners is likelier to let a base be stolen than one who is strong enough to do so.

Getting the Steal

It can be exciting to steal a base, but you need to know the right way to do it. Get a good jump off the bag while waiting for the bowler to throw. Focus on taking a quick first step and keeping your running speed up the whole steal. When getting close to second base, get ready to slide to avoid getting tagged. A downward slide is usually better because it lets you reach the bottom safely with your hand. Return to the base quickly and safely if the steal doesn't work. Do not find yourself in the wrong position.

Making Practice Better

To get good at intelligent base running, you have to train hard. Try taking leads off base and pretending to steal bases with a partner as the pitcher. Work on your secondary leads by practicing stealing an extra base and reacting to different pitchers throws. Do base running circuits, including hitting the ball, taking leads, rounding bases, and sliding.

Beyond the Basics: More Advanced Skills

The Hit and Run is a planned play in which the runner runs as soon as the ball is hit into play. This forces the defenders to make a quick play, which could lead to a score. With this move, you get a big lead and fake a steal attempt to get the pitcher to throw, which lets the hitter take a more significant swing. A runner gets ahead by a lot at first, but then they wait for the pitcher to throw home before they steal the base. This can take the defense off guard and give the offense a chance to score.

The Mental Game: More Than Technique

Smart baserunning uses your mind as well as your body. A good baserunner always has plans for the future. Plan out the plays, the pitcher's moves, and any mistakes the defense might make. On the basepaths, you need to make quick decisions. Do not think twice; follow your gut and respond to the situation. Do not be careless on the basepaths, but do be bold. You should know when to be bold and when to be safe.

You can go from being a passive watcher on the base paths to a strategic mastermind by developing situational solid awareness, aggressive base running skills, making intelligent decisions, and putting in a lot of practice. Defenses will fear you as a runner because you'll make them make quick choices all game long, putting pressure on them. Bright base running is more than just stealing bases. It's about using your knowledge, instincts, and athleticism to become a steady threat on the Field, changing the game's rules in your team's favor. Put on your cleats, learn the game, and master running bases. You'll make the defense look bad and bring your team one step closer to success.

Leveraging your arm strength

"Inoffensive situations."

In the right Field, having a strong arm isn't just about making a catch that will go down in history. That's a tool ready to be used, a force that can change the course of a game in your team's favor. But how do you turn raw arm strength into an edge on the offensive? Here's how to use your vast arm to become an offensive threat, making it hard for the other team's baserunners and giving your team chances to score.

How to Make a Strong Throw

There's more to a strong throw than just force. Pay attention to the right way to throw to get the most speed and accuracy. A good follow-through, a strong leg drive, and a smooth windup are all parts of this. Learn how to throw with different grips for different situations. A four-seam grip gives you the most speed and control, while a two-seam grip can make you move and trick more. Learn how to throw well with your feet. You can give your throw more power and speed by doing a solid crow hop or a controlled pivot step.

Keeping runners away

Baserunners may be scared off by your big arm, which can stop them from going for extra bases. Learn to let go of the ball quickly to keep runners close to the base. They might not want to steal or take a big lead if you throw quickly. Do not be scared to change things. Use fake throws at the right time to throw off baserunners and mess up their timing. This can make it easier for pickoffs or thefts to be caught. Stay in touch with your catcher and infielders at all times. Tell them what you plan to do and ensure everyone is on the same page. This will keep everyone from getting confused and wasting throws.

Creating Chances to Score

A strong arm isn't just good for protection; it can also be used to score. In a planned play, throw to the base as soon as the ball is hit into play. This forces the defenders to make a quick play, which could let the runner go an extra base. Your strong arm is essential if a baserunner gets caught in a rundown. Make exact throws to stop the runner and send him back to the base he was on before, giving you a chance to tag him out. When you're in right Field, you should back up throws from other outfielders, especially when the throw comes from deep left Field. When there are close plays at the plate or other bases, your strong arm can help get out.

Getting better at throwing

Training hard is needed to get a strong throwing arm. Add long toss drills to your routine, and as your arm strength improves, slowly increase the distance you throw. Pay attention to correct technique and accuracy. Throwing a medicine ball can help you get stronger in your arms and core. Try throwing differently to get faster and better at controlling your arm. Plyometric workouts make you more explosive, which means you can throw harder. Box jumps and squat jumps are good to add to your workout routine.

Mind Toughness: More Than Strength

It would help if you had a solid mind to have a strong arm. Trust your arm strength and your ability to make throws that change the game. With confidence, you can focus like a laser and make effective throws. Throwing quickly can happen when you're under a lot of stress. Keep calm and focus on the right tactics, even when things go badly. Try to figure out what went right and wrong with your throws. What went well? How could you have done it better? Use what you've learned to keep getting better at throwing accurately and effectively.

You can go from being an excellent right fielder with a good arm to an attacking force by learning the right way to throw, making innovative use of your arm strength, and toughening up mentally. Your throws will always be dangerous, changing how runners steal bases and giving your team chances to score. It's not enough to have a strong arm and make highlight-reel saves. You can also use your physical skills to change the game and scare your opponents with throwing power. Get better at what you do, let out your inner cannon, and be the right fielder who makes baserunners afraid by using your arm strength as a potent offensive tool.

CHAPTER 4

Speed, Agility, and Awareness

Exercises to enhance your speed

"And quickness."

Being fast and quick is essential for doing well in sports on the Field. These traits set great players apart from good ones, whether in the right Field chasing a fly ball, on base taking a base, or at bat hitting a fastball. But how do you get better at these hard-to-find skills? Rest assured that you can change from a slow mover to a blur of movement. Come with me as I go over a bunch of exercises that will make you faster and more agile, making you a real threat on the Field.

Building the Base: Power and Strength

Quickness and speed don't come together. To do strength training. It would help have strong legs, core, and upper body muscles for explosive moves. Do squats, lunges, deadlifts, and core work as your main workouts. Plyometrics teaches your muscles how to use all of their strength in a short amount of time. Box jumps, squat jumps, and depth jumps are some exercises you can add to your practice. These exercises are like the quick stops, starts, and changes of direction that you need to be able to do.

Developing Speed: Drills for Top Speed

Begin by sprinting as fast as you can for 20 to 30 meters. Ensure you have a solid first step, a good arm swing, and extended legs. Gradually extend the distance as you get faster. Practice the quick start you need to steal bases or chase fly balls. Focus on having quick reactions and a strong leg drive as you work on going from a controlled jog to an entire run. Hill sprints make your legs stronger and last longer. Find a hill with a modest slope and run as hard as you can up it. Start with short routes and slowly add more as your fitness level rises.

"Drills for Lightning-Fast Reactions" to Improve Speed

Speed is excellent, but you must quickly change directions and respond to new scenarios. Quickly move from side to side while keeping your feet on the ground and your body straight. Make sure you keep a good beat and change directions rapidly. Place cones in different shapes (L drills, star drills, etc.) and run around them quickly, focused on making sharp turns and staying in control. These drills will help you change directions more rapidly and without much trouble. Training your footwork with a speed ladder makes you more coordinated and quick. Focus on fast footwork and exact movements as you do drills like high knees, in-and-out steps, and lateral shuffles over the ladder.

For peak performance, do plyometrics to build explosive power.

Plyometric workouts take your speed and quickness to the next level by building your explosive power. Jump high onto a box, fall softly, and jump back down immediately. Start with a low box as you get better, and raise it as you go. Step off a stage (carefully!), land softly, and jump as high as you can immediately. For quick starts and direction changes, exercise helps your legs become more robust, and You jump as far as possible when you do broad jumps while standing up. Make sure you have a strong start and go horizontally as far as possible.

Beyond Drills: Why Rest and Recovery Are Important

Give your body enough time to rest and heal between workouts. This keeps you from hurting yourself and lets your muscles recover. Always do a dynamic warm-up before you train to prepare your muscles for quick moves and lower your risk of getting hurt. Do not push yourself too fast or too rigid. Listen to your body and take days off when necessary to prevent overtraining.

Making Drills Work for Game-Changing Performance

Drills for speed and quickness are only one part of the picture. Do drills like real games, stealing bases, responding to fly balls, etc. This helps you use the new skills you've learned in a stressful setting. Being fast and quick is as much a mental thing as it is a physical thing. Sharpen your attention and reaction time to predict plays and act on them without thinking. Regular exercise is critical. Please work on your speed and quickness, and do them regularly to see long-term results.

Making an All-Around Athlete

When you combine strength training, plyometrics, speed drills, agility drills, and the right way to heal, you'll go from being a hesitant athlete to a blur of controlled movement. Remember that quickness and speed are only two parts of being good at sports. Remember other essential skills, like accurately throwing, catching, and your baseball IQ.

Getting faster and more agile takes time, hard work, and patience. There will be days when things go wrong and progress seems slow. Enjoy your wins, no matter how big or small, and keep your mind on improving. You'll see your speed and agility turn into on-field success if you stick with it and work hard. Imagine how exciting it would be to steal a base with a bold slide, catch a deep fly ball in the outfield, or make a diving catch that saves the game. These things can happen if you train hard for speed and quickness. Put on your cleats, go out on the Field, and enjoy becoming faster, more agile, and a better baseball player. You don't have to be the fastest person on your team to be a speed demon. You must use your quickness and explosiveness to dominate the Field, leaving your opponents in the dust and leaving your mark on the game with every exciting play.

Reading the ball off the bat

"For efficient route running."

The sound of the bat hitting the ball and moving in a blur. When you play right Field, your heart beats fast. Where is the ball going? It takes skill to read the ball off the bat, which sets great outfielders apart from good ones. This is about turning that first blur into a plan that lets you find the best way to get to the ball and get out. Let's learn how to read the ball off the bat so you can go from being a nervous watcher to a smooth-running outfielder with laser focus.

The first look: initial exit speed and bat angle

When your bat hits the ball, you can start gathering information. A loud crack generally means the ball was hit harder. The ball will go deeper if it leaves the bat faster, so the first step needs to be faster, and the path needs to be more profound. The position of the bat when it hits the ball can help. When the arm is level, it looks like a line drive or a shallow fly ball. A higher uppercut swing could mean a high pop fly.

How to Understand the Hitter: Scouting and Recognizing Them

Getting to know your opponent can help you win. Look over scouting reports on the other team's hitters before the game. Learn about their power-hitting, pull-hitting style (hitting the ball toward right Field), and favorite swing mechanics. Watch the batter's body language and how they swing the bat while at bat. For a power swing, does he take a long step? For impact, does he take a short step? These small clues can help you figure out where the ball is going.

The First Read and the Crack of the Bat

It would be best to do something when you hear the bat hit the ball. A sharp, loud crack is often a sign of a line drive. Get ready for a quick start and a straight line to the ball. A dull thud could mean a ground ball or a pop fly. Look at the batter's swing and the bat's angle to figure out the expected path.

Following Through: Following the Ball as It Flies

You must watch the ball once it's in the air and change your play based on what you see. Keep your eyes on the ball's path and your head up. It's essential to keep your eyes on the ball and not check out your feet. It would help to change your path to get the best view as the ball moves. Don't run straight back to get to the ball faster; cut off angles as much as possible.

It's essential to communicate.

Baseball is played with other people. If the ball is hit far into centerfield, make your call loud and clear. This keeps people from running into each other and lets everyone know who is going for the catch. It's important to be ready to back up throws from other outfielders, especially on deep-fly balls, even if the ball isn't hit straight to you.

Making Practice Better

It takes skill and repetition to read the ball off the bat. Have a buddy hit fly balls or line drives with a fungo bat. These are called "front toss drills." Practice responding to the sound of the bat and getting to the ball correctly. Use a hitting machine that sends balls at different speeds and directions. Pay attention to reading the ball off the machine and taking the best routes. Do partner drills where someone on the other team calls out "line drive," "fly ball," or "ground ball" at random. This helps you train your reactions to respond quickly when you hear a word.

By knowing the hitter's hitting style, the bat angle, and the sound of the bat, you can turn that original blur into a map that shows you the way. As you work on your conversation, practice, and focus on following the ball as it moves, you'll become a right fielder known for quickly running routes and making plays on even the most brutal balls. It takes more than quick reflexes to read the ball off the bat. You must use your knowledge, anticipation, and attention to become a defensive force in the outfield. Get focused, step out onto the Field, and let the sound of the bat become your music. This will help you become a master of the outfield. Prepare for the crack and figure out the path, and with each successful route and safe out, you'll write your own story of defensive power on the baseball field.

Backing up other outfielders

"And understanding the situational play."

The noise of the crowd. A considerable line drive goes straight to Left Field. You tens up because you're the right fielder, and your eyes dart to the play. While the action happens elsewhere, you have an essential but often forgotten duty: help the other outfielders. What looks like a simple job can mean the difference between a routine out and an expensive extra-base hit. But backing up is more than just throwing; it's also about knowing what's going on in the game and changing how you play to fit it. Let's talk about how to be the best outfield teammate, which will turn you from a passive spectator into a defense chess master.

"The Art of the Backup: Making Sure You Cover All Your Bases"

When you back up, you look ahead for possible trouble spots and are ready to step in when needed. Know what you're supposed to do. You usually back up throws from left and centerfields when you're in right Field, especially when the ball is hit deep. It's important to talk to people all the time. Call for it clearly and loudly if the ball is hit toward you so you don't hit your friends. Going backward isn't a stroll. You should be ready to run as fast as possible to the possible play and be prepared to block throws or make a flying catch.

Figure out situational play and read the game like a pro.

You need to know what's happening in the game to back up nicely. If the game is close in the ninth, the backup pitcher needs to be bolder than if the game was a blowout in the second. When you have two outs, backing up is even more critical. It only takes one mistake on defense to change the outcome of a game. This is "The Hitter." Knowing how the batter usually hits the ball, you can guess where it will go. Does he hit for power and often sends balls far into the stands, or does he hit for contact and hit a lot of line drives all over the Field?

Beyond Basic Backups: More Advanced Methods

If there are men on base and a deep fly ball, the center and the right fielder might back up the throw from left Field. This makes for a more vigorous defense in case something goes wrong. "Playing the Wall" means moving closer to the wall when a fly ball is hit toward it in left or centerfield. This will stop any possible carom or home run. Even though it doesn't often happen, backing up on-ground balls hit by other outfielders can help prevent mistakes and possible passed balls.

Practice Makes Perfect: Backup Drills for Smooth Running

Play "Fly Ball Scenarios" with your friends by making them fake fly balls to different outfield parts. Practice blocking throws, talking clearly, and stopping throws that go off course. Work on backing up your throws when other outfielders hit ground balls.

Please pay attention to returning the ball to the infield and fielding it properly. Communication drills should be a part of your practice habit. Get better at working with your partners, calling for the ball, and using different hand signals.

You can go from being a passive observer to an active defensive player by learning how to back up and understand how the game is played. You become an extension of your friends, spotting problems before they happen and being there for them if something goes wrong. It's not about big plays that get attention; it's about quiet skill that keeps the game under control. You are my best friend, so be proud of that. Be the reliable right fielder that other players look to, the one who knows what will happen before it does, and the one whose intelligent choices lead to outs and wins. You can become a defensive genius, a silent guardian of the outfield, and a real benefit to your baseball team if you work hard and keep your eye on the big picture.

CHAPTER 5

MENTAL RESILIENCE IN RIGHT FIELD

Staying focused

"Throughout the game."

Baseball is not a sprint, it's a journey. The difference between good and great players is their ability to keep their minds on the game during long games with many ups and downs in the fight. Most of the time that missed catch on a routine fly ball in the ninth inning was caused by losing focus. Here are some ways to build mental toughness and stay focused during the game to play your best from the first pitch to the last out.

The Foundation: Getting Ready Before the Game

A clear head starts a long time before the first pitch. Picture yourself doing well. Think about making regular plays like hitting line drives and catching fly balls. Visualizing good things boosts your confidence and gets your mind ready to succeed. Focusing on mistakes or harmful thoughts from the past can make it hard to see the present. Instead, talk positively to yourself to feel better and stay in the present. Having a routine before a game helps you calm down and concentrate. For example, you could stretch, listen to music, or work on your throws with a partner.

Being Mindful in the Field: Staying Present

A lot of things can distract you during the game. Don't think about mistakes you've made or what might happen. Pay close attention to the play that is happening right now. Taking deep breaths can help you deal with stress and stay focused. If you can't handle everything, take a few deep breaths to calm down. Block out outside noises like the crowd or the scores. Pay attention to the game sounds and how your friends are talking to each other.

Keeping Your Focus During Downtime

Let's be honest: baseball does have slow times. Don't just zone out between rounds. To keep yourself busy, jog in place, stretch, or practice your swing in the shadows. When you have some free time, go over future events in your mind. Think about what it would be like to catch a ground ball, steal a base, or throw a fundamental pitch. Support your team and keep your mind on the game. A positive and helpful mood helps you stay focused and boosts team spirit.

How to Deal with Stress and Setbacks

Lots of people have bad games. Don't think about mistakes all the time. Please take what you learned from them and move on to the next pitch or play. Think about the good things about your game. Enjoy your wins, no matter how small they are: a great catch, a solid throw to the plate, or a hard-hit ball. "Trust Your Training" means remembering all the hard work and commitment you put into practice. Have faith in your skills; know you've been preparing for this.

Mental Toughness: Getting Your Mind Clear

Getting mentally tough is essential for staying focused. Mindfulness meditation and other types of meditation can help you concentrate and keep your thinking in check. Look at mishaps as chances to learn and get better. Figure out what went wrong and use that information to improve your thoughts about the next game. Believe that you can get better at sports and mentally tough through hard work and commitment.

"Staying Focused: It Takes a Team"

Focusing isn't something you can do by yourself. Cheer your friends on and help them succeed. Giving people praise boosts their confidence and keeps them on task. Have good conversations with your teammates. This keeps everyone on the same page and clears up any confusion, making the space more focused. Good team leaders set the tone for a lot of work and attention. Their hard work and concentration can motivate their friends to keep going strong during the game.

If you follow these tips, you'll go from being a player who often loses focus to a focused rival. You'll be ready for the game, able to stay in the present, and easily handle distractions. It would help if you worked out your mental toughness like a muscle. Focus is something you can develop through hard work and practice. This will help you perform at your best throughout the game and help your team win every pitch and play. Go out onto the Field with a clear head, a focused gaze, and the unrelenting drive to beat everyone else. Let your attention be your weapon. A laser-like focus can distinguish between a regular play and one that changes the game. You have to think about things when you play baseball. You'll go from being an excellent right fielder to a great one if you learn to stay focused. Your friends will depend on you, and you'll be a force to be reckoned with on the diamond.

Handling pressure

"And big moments with composure."

There are two outs at the bottom of the ninth, and the bases are total. The stadium is rocking with the sound of the bat hitting the ball. As the ball speeds toward the gap, all eyes are on you, the right fielder. Your heart beats fast, and adrenaline speeds up. Now is the time you've been training for, but stress can be harmful. It can either hurt your success or make it better. Here's how to stay calm under pressure to shine in big games and become a player who does well in front of the camera.

Get to Know Yourself

Being aware of yourself is the first step. How do you usually handle stress? Do you get tighter, or does it help you concentrate better? Figuring out your habits enables you to devise ways to deal with them. Deep breathing and positive self-talk can help some people feel better. Others might do better by picturing themselves making the catch that wins the game.

Enjoy the Moment

Don't run away from stress. See it as a chance to step up to the challenge. Don't forget that the other team is also under fire. Focus on it like a laser instead of letting it dominate you. Use the rush of energy to improve your reactions and reflexes.

Pay attention to the play.

It's simple to get caught up in how big the moment is. Don't forget, though, that it's still just baseball. Don't overthink about what might happen if you make a mistake. Your attention should be focused on the job at hand instead. What does tracking the fly ball, making a clean catch, or throwing a strike to the batter mean? Pay attention to doing the basics perfectly.

Believe in Your Training

You weren't supposed to be here. Remember all the practice hours you put in to get better. Trust the training and planning you've done. Your muscles will remember what to do when you need them the most.

Rules are your friend.

Even when things are stressful, stick to your pre-game habits. It's nice to feel at ease when you do things that are familiar to you. These habits, like listening to your favorite upbeat song or picturing yourself succeeding, can help you calm down and get back on track.

"Learn from Your Mistakes"

Everybody messes up sometimes. Even the best players miss a crucial ground ball or strike out when the bases are total. Don't think about the past too much. Determine what went wrong, take what you've learned, and move on. Pay attention to the next ball, play, and chance to make things right.

Good reinforcement

Pay attention to the good things about your game. Did you do something great early in the game? Did you hit a line drive close to the foul pole but not quite? Enjoy your wins, no matter how small they are. This boosts confidence and helps you keep an upbeat attitude.

It takes a team to make a dream come true.

Baseball is played with other people. Use your friends to help you. A supportive pat on the back or a word of support from a friend can help you feel better and remember that you're not alone.

You can go from being a player who falls apart in big moments to shining when it matters by accepting pressure, staying focused, and believing in your preparation. Being calm is a skill that can be learned. Your team will look to you when the game is on the line and the stakes are high. With hard work and practice, you'll become the player who keeps their cool and helps them win.

Building mental strength

"And a positive mindset."

Baseball isn't just about how strong you are; it's also a fight of wills. Most of the time, the player with the best mental game wins. Here are some ways to build mental strength and a positive attitude that will help you go from being a good player to a winner on the Field.

Self-belief and confidence are the building blocks of a strong foundation.

Self-belief is the first thing that builds mental strength. Don't think about the things you've done wrong in the past. Enjoy your wins, no matter how big or small they are. Did you catch something great? Did you get a line drive? Recognize the things you've done well and have faith in your skills. Say good things to yourself instead of negative things. Not "I can't do this," but "I can" or "I'm going to give it my all." Positive self-talk helps you feel more confident and fights doubt. Picture yourself doing well. Think about jumping to make that catch, hitting that double that wins the game, or throwing a strike to the batter. Visualization can help you train your mind to do well.

Getting more assertive and more determined

Don't let your mistakes define who you are. Determine what went wrong, take what you've learned, and move on. You can control how hard you work, how focused you are, and how you feel. See problems as chances to learn and grow. Hard times test your mental toughness and help you become more resilient. Believe that you can improve if you work hard and keep at it. Don't just focus on getting results immediately; learn and grow.

How to Keep a Positive Attitude

It's easy to spread a good mood, on and off the Field. Don't overthink about the past or the future. Keep your attention on the play that is happening right now. Be thankful that you can play the game you love. Having a good mood lowers your stress and makes the game more fun. Be a good example for your coworkers. Please help keep the team spirit upbeat by cheering them on and celebrating their wins.

Exercises for Mental Training

Mental skills need to be trained just like your muscles. Mindfulness meditation and other types of meditation can help you concentrate and deal with stress. Writing down your goals and thoughts can help you see harmful patterns and change your attitude. Picture yourself doing well in games regularly.

Building mental strength and a positive attitude is a process that never ends. Things will go wrong, and problems will come up along the way. You can change how you play the game by working on mental training, having faith in yourself, being strong, and having a good attitude. As a player, you'll learn how to handle stress, motivate your team, and have the spirit of a true winner. Being mentally strong isn't just about winning; it's also about being ready for challenges, learning from mistakes, and playing the game with heart and purpose. When you step onto the Field, you should have a clear head, a good attitude, and a strong desire to be the best player you can be.

CHAPTER 6

READY FOR GAME DAY

A solid pre-game routine

The sound of the bat hitting the ball. The noise of the crowd. As I step onto the Field, my heart is racing with excitement. However, a straightforward pre-game practice prepares you to perform at your best before the game starts. This personalized ritual calms your nerves, helps you concentrate, and gets your body and mind ready to win the race. Here are some tips for making a pre-game routine that will turn you from a worried spectator into a confident player.

The foundation: the things that make up your routine

You can't use the same method for everyone. Your routine before a game should be based on what you like and what you need. Close your eyes and picture yourself doing your best. Think about jumping to catch balls, hitting line drives, and throwing strikes. You can train your mind to be successful and boost your confidence by visualizing. Focusing on mistakes or harmful thoughts from the past can make it hard to see the present. It's better to say good things like "I am focused," "I am prepared," or "I trust my training." Talking positively to yourself fights doubt and helps you think like a winner. It would be best to do an active warm-up to prepare your body for the game. Light jogging, stretches for your core and throwing arm, and workouts that make you more agile and flexible should all be part of your routine. Include drills that are similar to the way you move on the Field. This could mean doing drills for right fielders to track fly balls, catch pop flies, and make outfield throws. Music can help you focus and get in the zone. Pick upbeat, inspiring songs to get you pumped up and help you concentrate.

Making changes to your routine: figuring out what works for you

A pre-game practice is great because it can be changed to fit your needs. Do you like having a set schedule or being able to change things up? Test things out to see what works best for you. Don't have a lot of time before the game? Pay attention to the most critical parts of your practice, like doing light stretches and telling yourself nice things. Think about adding team-building events to your schedule. They will help you work together and feel like a group.

Getting into the habit of doing the same thing every day

A pre-game practice is most useful when done the same way every time. Set aside time for your pre-game practice and ensure you have enough time to do it without rushing. Don't make significant changes on game day if you've already set up a pattern. Being consistent helps your body and mind change and get ready. During pre-season practice, you can start to build your schedule. This allows you to make changes and ensure they work well before the games begin.

How a pre-game routine can change things from routine to outcome

A transparent process before a game can make all the difference. It calms your nerves before the game, helps you concentrate, and prepares your body to do its best. In addition, your routine turns into a known safe space, a place in your mind where you can calm down and feel ready to play.

Your routine before a game is a journey for you. Try different things until you find the one that works best for you. Your pre-game routine will take you from being a good player to a great one if you stick with it. The next time you step onto the diamond, you'll be ready to rule the Field.

Scouting reports

"And understanding the opposition."

When you play baseball, you need to know your opponent well to win. This is where research reports are helpful; they tell you much about the teams you'll be playing. But how do you turn that info into knowledge that you can use? Let's look into scouting reports and show you how to read them. This will give you the edge you need to win on the Field.

What Scouting Reports Show About the Power of Information

Professionals spend much time researching their future opponents and writing scouting reports. Learn about the good and bad habits of each batter. A lot of the time, do they pull the ball to right Field? Do they hit for power, or do they hit for contact and hit a lot of line drives? Know the different types of pitches your team will face. Do they depend on breaking pitches and fastballs? Are they known to throw hard hits, or are they crazy? If you're playing baseball, you should know whether the other team steals bases fiercely or more cautiously. This information could change where you stand in the center. Scouting reports may show the preferred defensive shifts of the other team, which lets you guess where the batter might hit the ball based on the situation and the batter.

Decoding the Data: How to Use Scout Reports to Your Advantage

Scout reports are helpful, but they are just numbers. "Internalize the Information" means to read the whole report, not just skim it. Focus on the most critical information for your role as you take the time to learn about each player's habits. For instance, a right fielder should closely examine how batters usually hit and where a fly ball might land. Scout logs are an excellent place to begin. Watch the other team's players in action during batting practice or warm-ups before the game. This can show you more information, like a batter's stance or a pitcher's movements, which will help you understand even better. Don't be afraid to talk to your teachers about the scouting report. They can give you information specific to your job on the diamond, giving you insights and interpretations.

After Reading the Report: Trust Your Gut

Even though scouting reports are helpful, they shouldn't replace your feelings in the game. Do not be afraid to change where you are standing, depending on the game. For instance, if runners are on base, you might play more profoundly in the center to stop hits over the fence. A hitter might surprise you by hitting the ball in a way that is different from what the report says. Trust your sensory cues and act based on what you see. Talk to your friends while the game is going on. Let your infielders know when a batter seems to favor one side of the Field over the other.

You have a significant edge on the Field if you know how to use scouting reports well. You see how the pitcher throws and can change your position based on what you think the batter will do. Accounts from scouts are only one part of the picture. You can be successful if you use these tips, observe the game, trust your gut, and talk to your team. You'll be ready to beat your opponent and win the baseball game when you step onto the Field with new knowledge and the ability to understand the game.

Emphasizing recovery

"Nutrition, and optimal health."

It's not enough to hit home runs and make excellent saves in baseball. It's a marathon, not a race, so you must keep working out to get in the best shape possible. Recovery, nutrition, and general health are the unsung heroes that make your on-field success possible. Here's how to put these critical things in order of importance and go from being a weekend warrior to a well-oiled machine on the Field.

The Power of Recovery: How to Rest Your Body to Perform at Its Best

Playing baseball is hard on your body. Overuse injuries can happen when you throw too much, making your muscles tired and your joints hurt. Aim for 7-8 hours of sound sleep every night. During sleep, your body heals itself, gets more energy, and strengthens your defense system. Don't stop working out after the game. Set aside time to do stretches focusing on the main muscle groups you used during the game. On days when you don't have a game, doing light activities like walking, swimming, or yoga can help your blood flow, which helps your muscles heal and makes them less sore.

Fire Up Your Machine: The Best Foods for Baseball Performance

What you eat makes you who you are. What you eat directly affects your health, energy level, and muscle power. A healthy diet of fruits, veggies, and whole grains is essential. These give your body the vitamins, minerals, and complex carbs to keep going during long games. To heal and grow muscles, you need a lot of protein. Chicken, fish, beans, and lentils are all lean protein sources that you should eat. Water is necessary for good function. During the day, especially before, during, and after games, drink a lot of water. Please avoid sugary drinks because they can make you tired and dehydrated. Make a plan for your food. Meals before a game should be high in complex carbs to give you lasting energy. To help muscles heal, meals after a game should include a lot of protein and carbs.

Going Beyond the Basics: Improving Your Health for Overall Wellness

Peak performance is more than just eating right and recovering. Add exercises for strength training to your schedule. This strengthens muscles, boosts power, and lowers the risk of getting hurt. Take care of your pain. If you have pain or soreness that won't disappear, take care of it before it worsens. If you need to, don't be afraid to get medical help. A healthy mind goes well with a healthy body. Mind exercises, like visualization or meditation, can help you concentrate better, deal with worry better, and feel better all around. It can be hard to handle baseball. Spending time with loved ones, learning to relax, or doing things you enjoy are all excellent ways to deal with stress.

Creating a Long-Term Way of Life: Making Healthy Habits Stick

Make healthy habits a part of your daily life for baseball success, not just something you do on game day. There isn't a single way to do things that works for everyone. Try different ways to recover, such as different diets and workout plans. Discover what suits your body and tastes the best. Start small and add good habits to your daily life over time. Your chances of success increase if you set goals that you can reach—having friends, family, or a coach to help you can hold you responsible and keep you going when things get tough.

You can go from being a tired player to a well-oiled machine on the Field by putting recovery, nutrition, and general health first. You'll get better faster, have more energy, and be less likely to get hurt. A healthy body is a happy body that works at its best. Put your health first, give your body what it needs to do well, and go out on the Field with the confidence and energy of a real winner. You can reach your full potential, dominate the game, and become your best player if you work hard and pledge to healthy living.

Closing Thoughts

Remember as you close this book that being a great right fielder is more than just being able to throw and catch fly balls. Focusing on the mind, being physically strong, and promising to stick to good habits are all part of a whole-person approach. Take on the task of becoming a complete player. Focusing on visualization exercises will improve your brainpower; eating well and getting enough sleep will fuel your body for top performance. Remember that the only way to become a winner is to work hard, be dedicated, and always try to get better. Feel more sure of yourself as you step onto the ground. Focus like a laser, throw like a rocket, and use your game knowledge to your advantage. Baseball is both a mental and a physical game of chess. Now that you know these tips, you can beat your opponents. The right fielder may not be the star of every play, but they are critical to the team's success. Take care of the outfield without being seen. Your friends depend on you, and you'll do well under pressure. It would help if you shone because the diamond is waiting for you.